Little Pebble™

Farm Facts

Buildings
on the Farm

by Lisa J. Amstutz

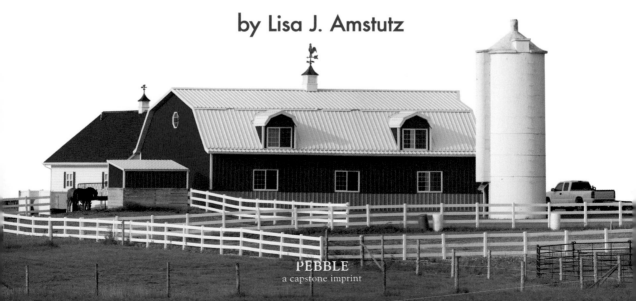

PEBBLE
a capstone imprint

Pebble Books are published by Pebble
1710 Roe Crest Drive
North Mankato, Minnesota 56003
www.mycapstone.com

Library of Congress Cataloging-in-Publication Data
is available on the Library of Congress website.
ISBN 978-1-9771-0258-4 (library binding)
ISBN 978-1-9771-0538-7 (paperback)
ISBN 978-1-9771-0263-8 (eBook PDF)
Summary: Introduces beginning readers to some
of the most common buildings found on a farm
and what they're used for, including barns,
chicken coops, stables, and more.

Editorial Credits
Jill Kalz, editor; Ashlee Suker, designer;
Kelly Garvin, media researcher;
Katy LaVigne, production specialist

Photo Credits
Ashlee Suker, 19; iStockphoto: chuckcollier ,
backcover, 10, JamesBrey 1, 7, 12, nullplus 9,
SimplyCreativePhotography 15; Shutterstock:
Arina P. Habich, 11, Brenda Carson, 8, James.
Pintar, cover, Johnny Adolphson, 21, LEE SNIDER
PHOTO IMAGES, 5, Lucian Milasan, 13, Tom Mc
Nemar, 17, tongcom photographer, 20

Design Element
Shutterstock: Dudarev Mikhail, J.Schelkle,
K.Narloch-Liberra, laura.h, Sichon

Printed and bound in China.
996

Table of Contents

On the Farm

Farms have many buildings. Each one holds something special. Let's look!

Places for Animals

A barn keeps farm animals safe and dry. You can find cows in a barn. *Moo!*

Farmers store straw
and hay in barns.

Some farm animals eat hay.

Many sleep on straw.

STRAW

HAY

Cluck! Cluck!

Hens live in a chicken coop.

They lay eggs in nest boxes.

A stable is a big barn.

You can find horses here.

Each horse has a stall.

Other Places

A silo is tall and round.

Farmers store grain in it.

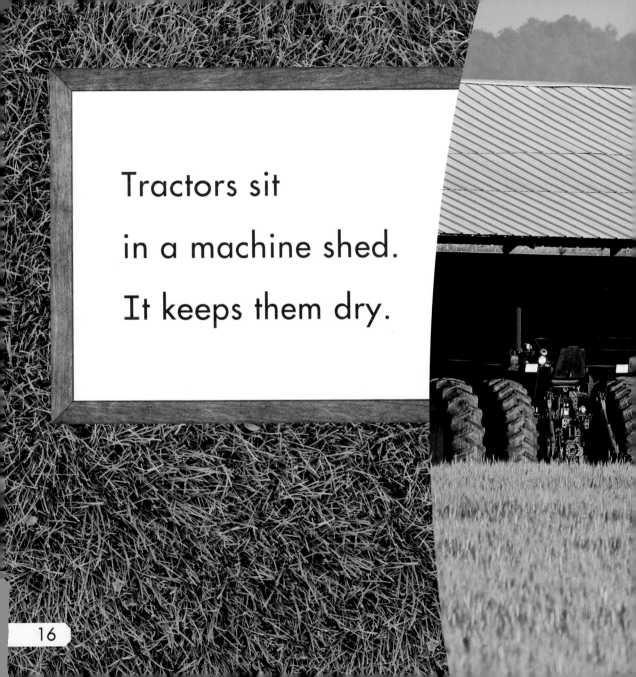

Tractors sit
in a machine shed.
It keeps them dry.

Oh no! The tractor broke!

The tools are

in the tool shed.

This is a farmhouse.

Who lives here?

Farmers do!

Glossary

barn—a farm building where crops, animals, and equipment are kept

grain—the seed of a grassy plant such as wheat, rice, corn, rye, or barley

hay—dried field grasses

machine—a piece of equipment that is used to do a job

shed—a simple building used for storage

silo—a tall, round tower used to store food for farm animals

stable—a building where horses are kept

stall—the area of a stable where a horse sleeps

straw—dried stems of wheat, barley, or oat plants

Read More

Borth, Teddy. *Buildings on the Farm.* On the Farm. Minneapolis: Abdo Kids, 2015.

Hoena, Blake A. *The Farm: a 4D Book.* A Visit to … North Mankato, Minn.: Capstone Press, 2018.

Kelley, K.C. *Farm.* Field Trips, Let's Go! Mankato, Minn.: Amicus, 2018.

Internet Sites

Use FactHound to find Internet sites related to this book.

Visit *www.facthound.com*

Just type in 9781977102584 and go.

Check out projects, games and lots more at
www.capstonekids.com

Critical Thinking Questions

1. What are three buildings you may find on a farm?

2. Why are barns useful on a farm?

3. What do you think is the most important farm building? Why?

Index